Early Learn

Sticker Act

ABC

priddy books
big ideas for little people

Aa

Apple, ax and astronaut - what other words begin with "a"?

apple

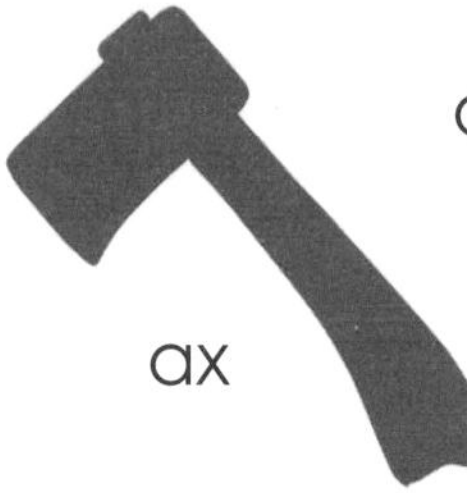

ax

astronaut

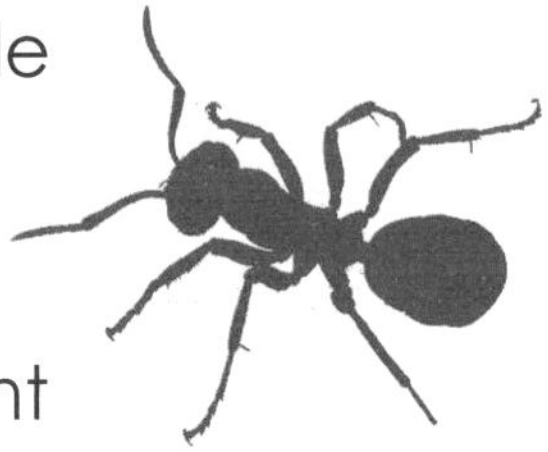

ant

Where would you travel to if you were an astronaut?

Bb

What insect flies and goes "buzz, buzz"? Can you find something else that flies?

baby

butterfly

What other "b" words do you see?

bulldozer

bumblebee

Cc

What do you think each of these objects feels like?

coconut

Which of these turns into a butterfly?

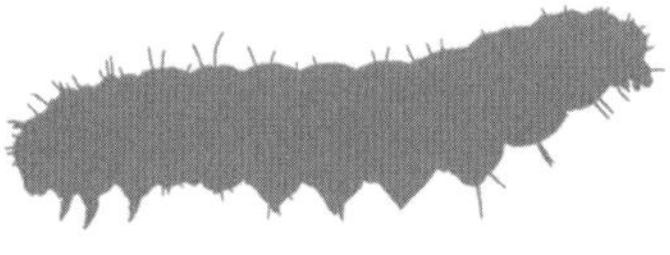

caterpillar

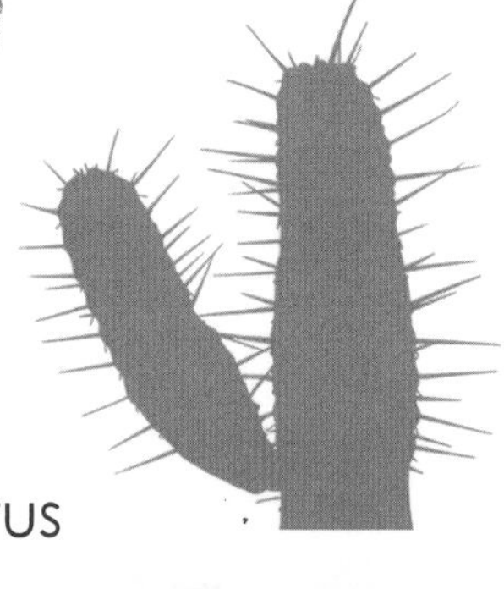

cactus

cat

doll

dalmatian

dinosaur

Which animal lived millions of years ago?

D d

Can you find a black and white dog? What is this type of dog called?

earth

egg

envelopes

elephant

What planet do we live on?

E e

How many words beginning with "e" can you see here?

Can you find an animal with stripes that swims?

fish

flag

friends

F f

How many people are in your family? Do any of their names begin with "F"?

Gg

Which "g" is juicy, sweet and delicious to eat?

goat

grapes

girl

Who's making a silly face - the goat or the girl?

Hh

How many windows does this house have?

What "h" has five fingers?

house

hand

Ii

Which "i" is hot and which "i" is cold?

iron

ice cream

Don't ever touch a hot iron!

iguana

Jj

Which of these things can't you eat?

What can you put on your toast that begins with "j"?

juice

jelly

jeans

What do you use to open your front door?

kettle

keys

koala

Kk

Can you find two shiny objects that begin with "k"?

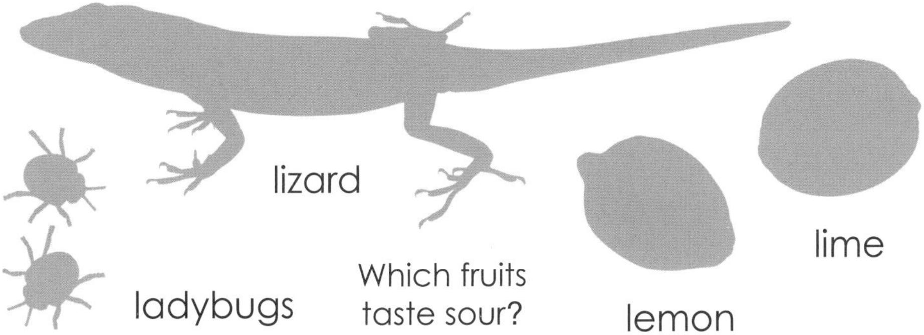

lizard

ladybugs

Which fruits taste sour?

lemon

lime

Ll

Does a lizard prefer to eat lemons or ladybugs?

motorcycle

Can you think of any other "m" words?

Mm

How many "m"s are in the word "mommy"?

Do you know which number comes next?

1 2 3 4

5 6 7 8

numbers

Nn

How old are you? Is your age one of these numbers?

Oo

What noise does an owl make?

Which vegetable makes your eyes water?

orange

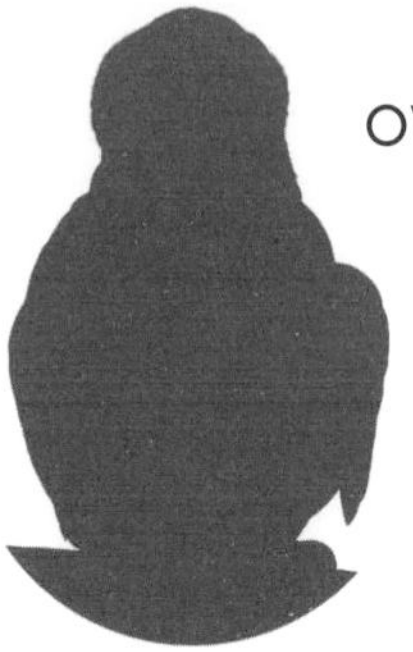

owl

onions

Pp

What colors begin with the letter "p"?

parrot

How many peas are in this pod?

peas

painter

Qq

Would you put a quiche or a quilt on your bed?

What can you eat that begins with "q"?

quilt

quiche

Rr

What other animals begin with the letter "r"?

rainbow

Can you name these colors?

raspberries

rabbit

Ss

spade

seagull

starfish

How many of these are found at the beach?

spider

What other "s" words can you find by the sea?

Tt

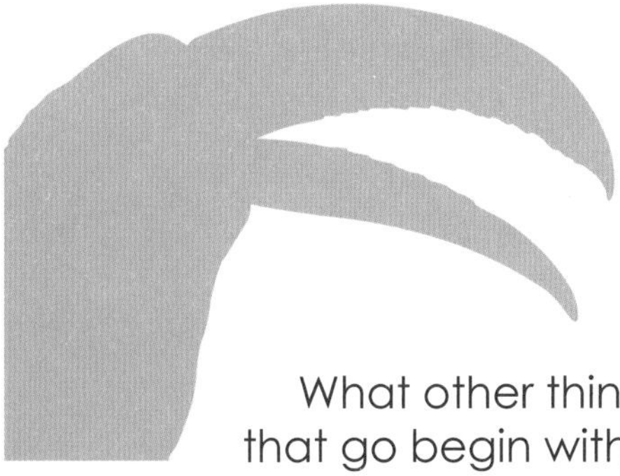

toucan

truck

What other things that go begin with "t"?

What "t" do you show when you smile?

Uu

When would you use an umbrella?

umbrella

undress

under

What's the opposite of "down"?

Vv

What vegetables do you like to eat?

vegetables

What letters do these vegetables begin with?

Ww

What would you put in a watering can?

wolf

wheelbarrow

watering can

Which of these belong in the yard?

Xx

What kind of pictures are taken at hospitals?

What sound does the "x" in xylophone make?

xylophone

Yy

What color beginning with "y" is the sun?

What toy goes up and down?

yawn

yo-yo

yacht

Zz

Does a zebra have stripes or spots?

zebra

Where would you see a zebra?

zigzags

See if you can find out where these letter stickers belong.

a b c d e

f g h i j

k l m n o

p q r s t u

v w x y z

Aa Bb Cc Dd Ee

cat

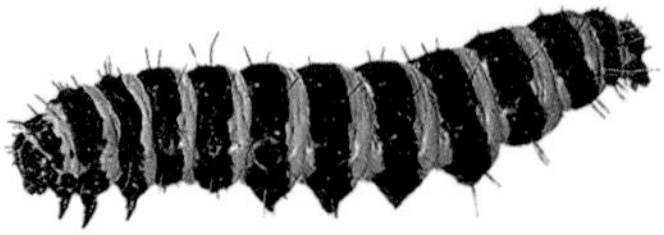

caterpillar

butterfly

astronaut

ax

Earth

bulldozer

ant

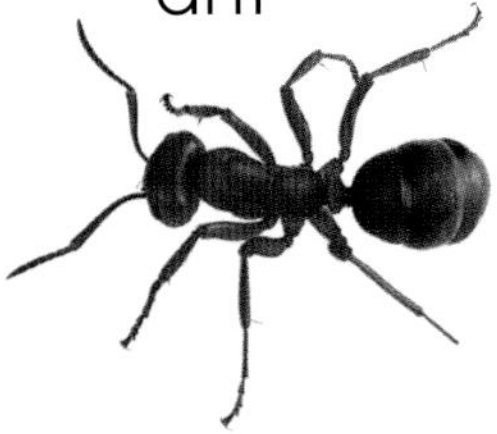

envelopes

dinosaur

cactus

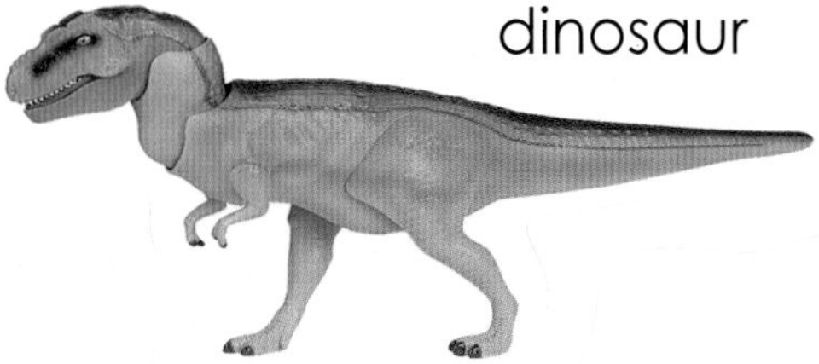

doll

coconut

dalmatian

bumblebee

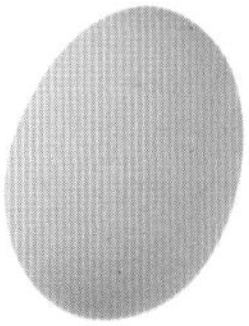

egg

apple

elephant

baby

Ff Gg Hh Ii Jj

ice cream

jelly

house

friends

goat

fish

iguana

jeans

grapes

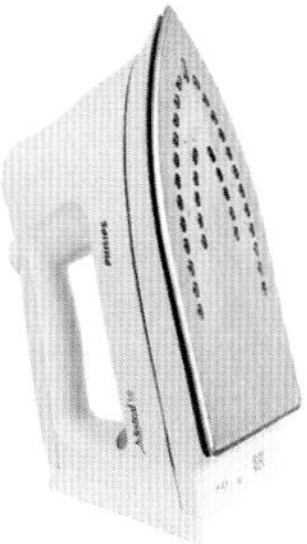

iron

flag

juice

girl

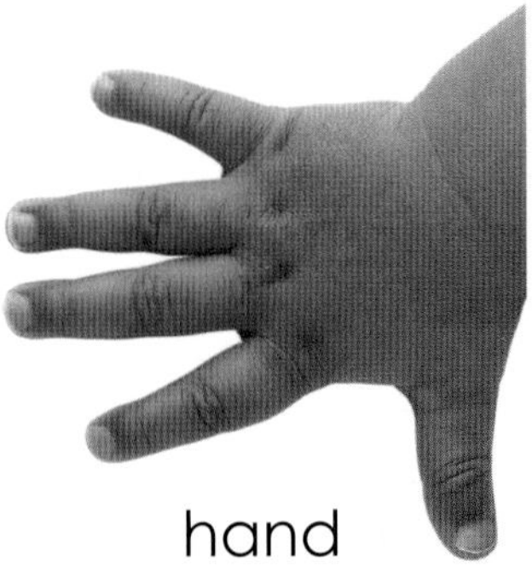

hand

Kk Ll Mm Nn Oo

lizard

owl

onions

keys

ladybugs

orange

koala

kettle

lemon

lime

motorcycle

1 2 3 4
5 6 7 8

numbers

Pp Qq Rr Ss Tt

toucan

painter

rabbit

raspberries

peas

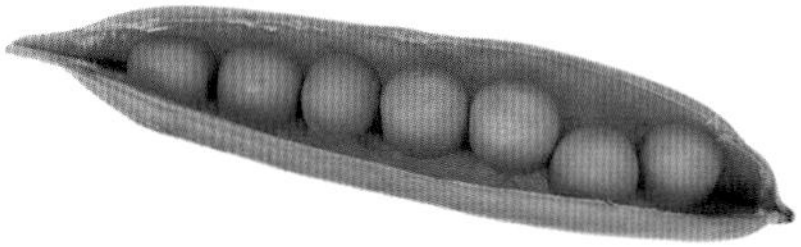

starfish

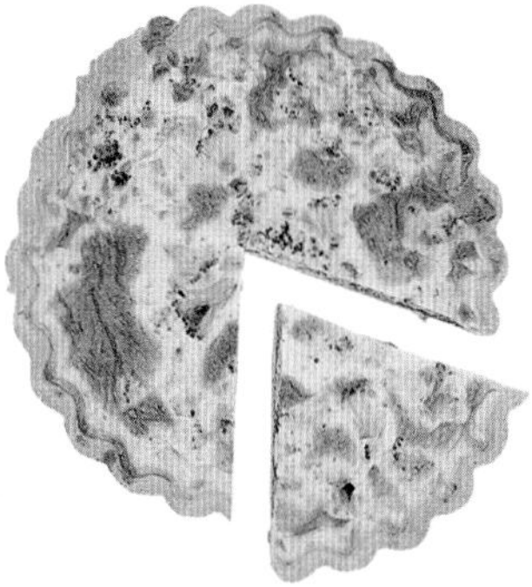

quiche

spade

seagull

parrot

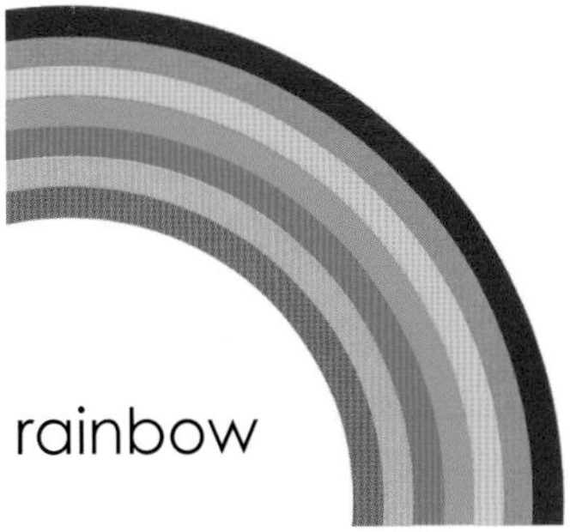

rainbow

spider

quilt

truck

Uu Vv Ww Xx Yy Zz

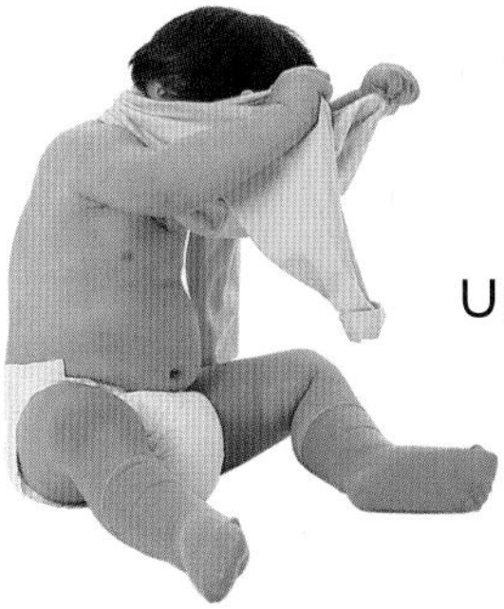

undress

umbrella

vegetables

yo-yo

xylophone

watering can

yawn

yacht

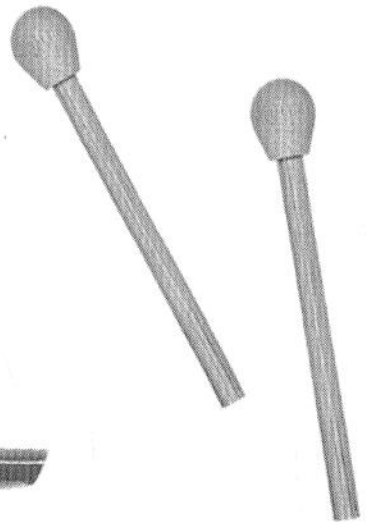

wolf

zebra

zigzags

under

wheelbarrow

A a

apple

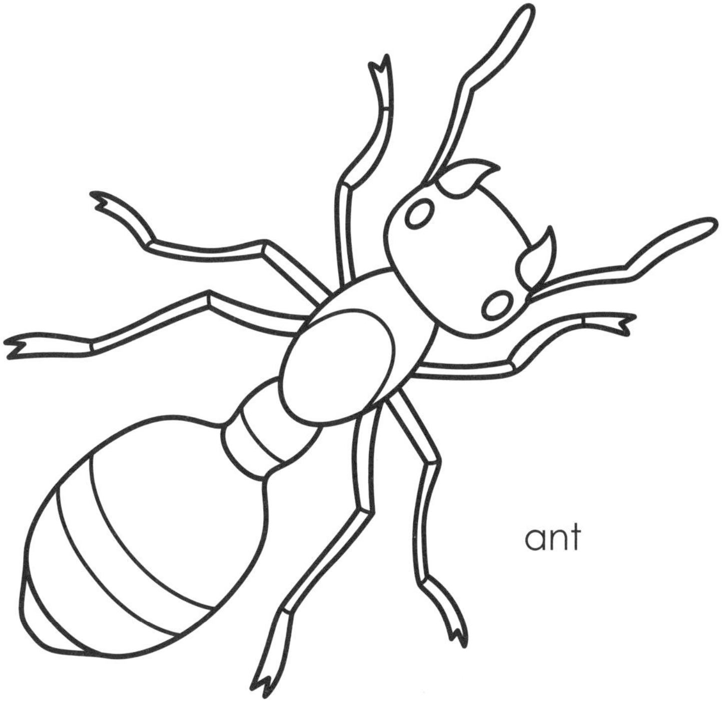

ant

B b

butterfly

bumblebee

Cc

cat

chicken

Dd

drum

dinosaur

Earth

elephant

Ee

fire truck

Ff

frog

Gg

giraffe

grapes

Hh

hippopotamus

horse

I i

ice cream

igloo

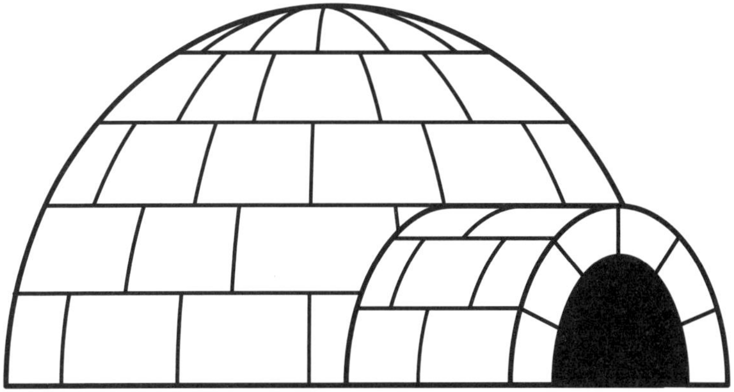

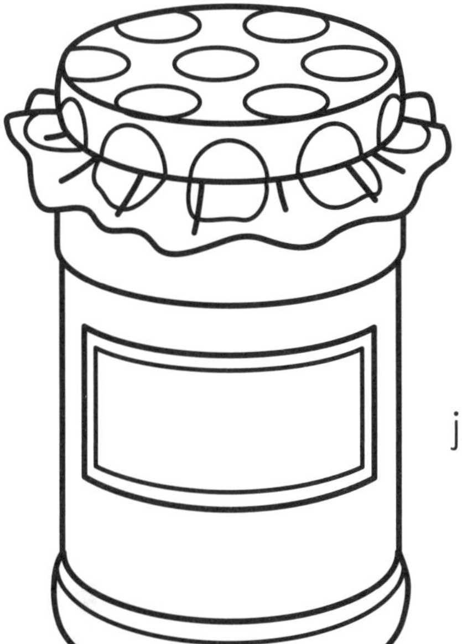

jelly

J j

jigsaw
puzzle

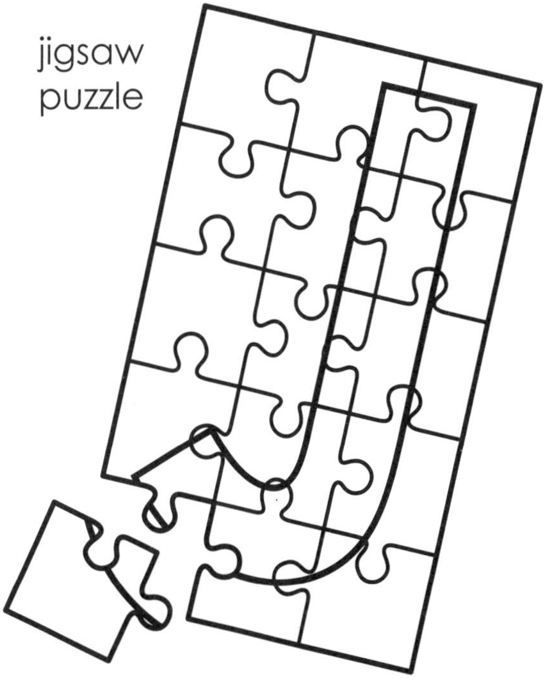

Kk

kettle

koala

Ll

ladybug

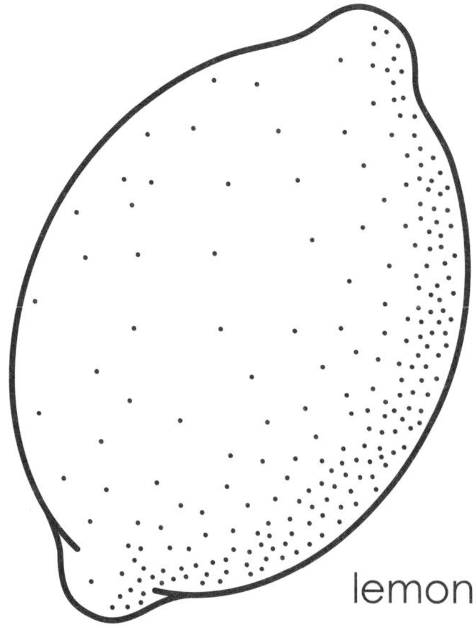

lemon

mouse

motorcycle

Mm

numbers

nest

Nn

Oo

owl

Pp

penguin

pencils

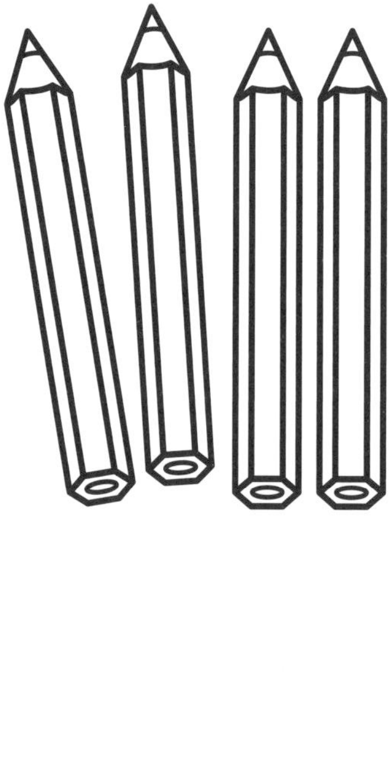

Qq

queen

Rr

rabbit

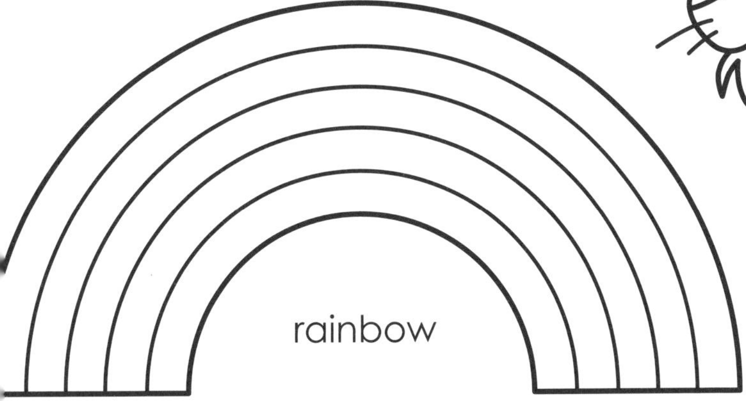

rainbow

Ss

sunflower

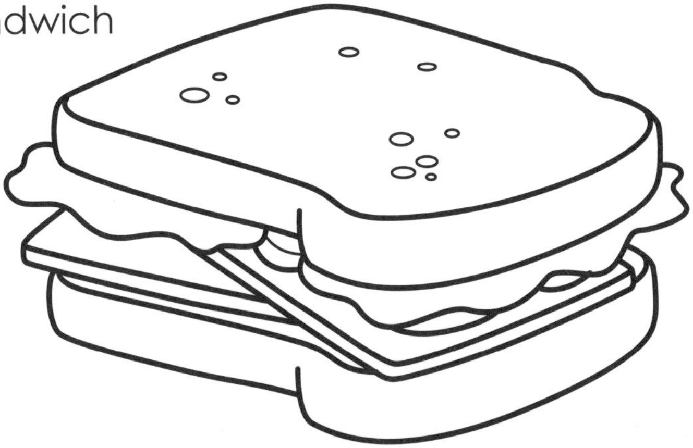

sandwich

T t

train

tiger

U u

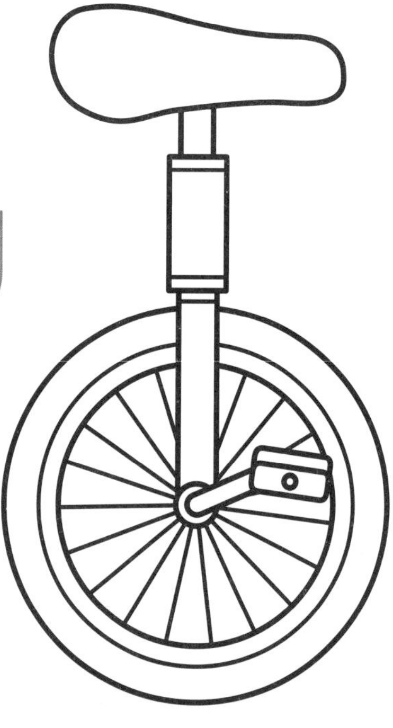

umbrella

unicycle

Vv

violin

vegetables

Ww

watering
can

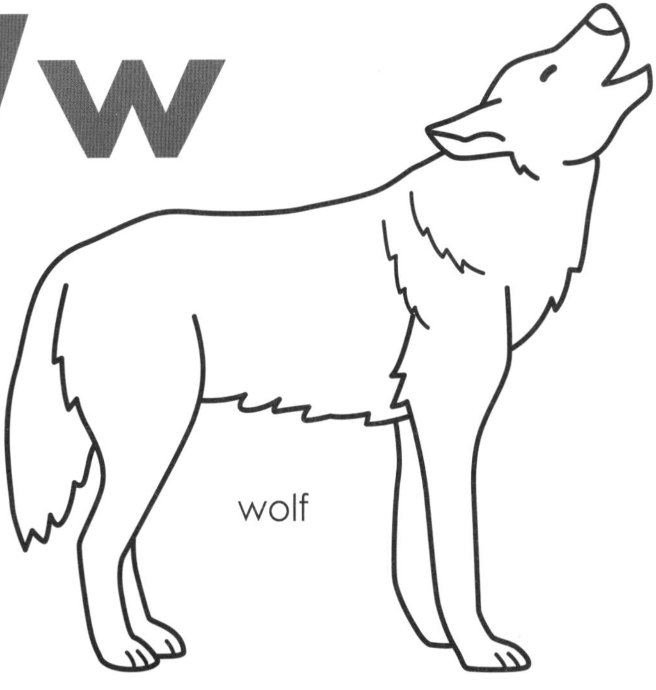

wolf

Xx

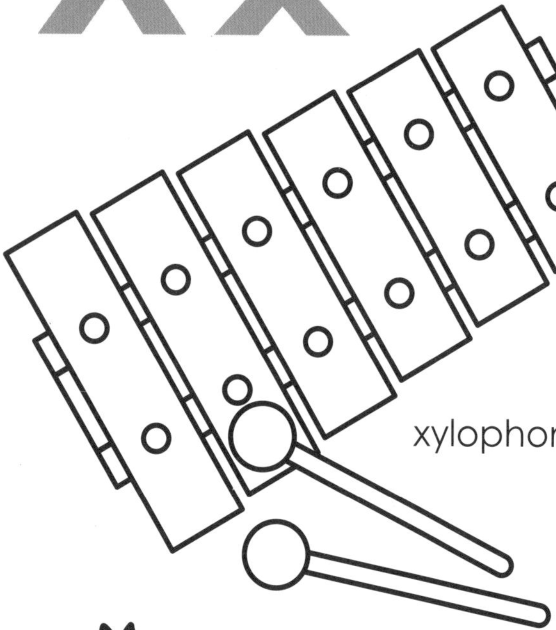

xylophone

yo-yo

Yy

yacht

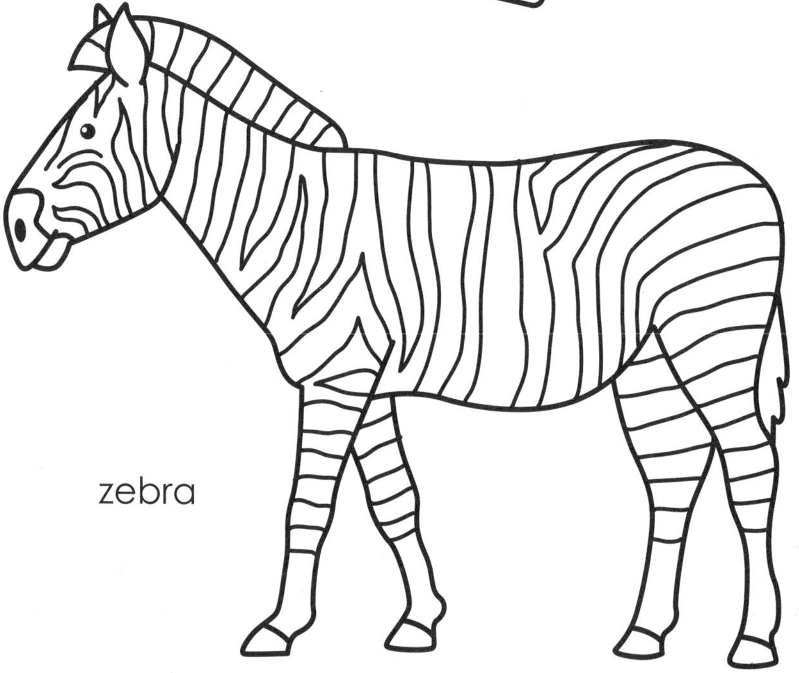

zebra

Zz

zigzag